Easy to Read

Seventeen Syllables

Haiku Poems

A Journey Through The Four Seasons

Muriel A Kingsley

Emerald Torrus Publishers

A catalogue record for this book is available from the British Library.

Paperback - ISBN 9781068656514

Published by Emerald Torrus Publishers
Edited by Barrina Mills

info@emeraldtorrus.com

About the Author

Muriel was born in Jamaica in 1943. She began school at seven and finished at twelve, barely able to write her own name. At the age of twenty-six, she moved to England, still with limited writing skills and only able to read a few Bible verses.

Unable to read fluently at the age of forty, Muriel joined adult education classes in Wandsworth, London. With the encouragement of her six children and teachers, she embarked on a journey to improve her reading skills and communicate effectively through writing.

Her initial qualification was a City & Guilds certificate in Cookery, which opened the door for her to work as a cook in a private nursing home.

At fifty-two, due to health reasons, Muriel retired. She returned to adult learning, exploring a variety of courses including maths, English, dressmaking, pottery, and watercolour painting. She continued to study at South Thames College in Wandsworth, later attending Croydon Adult Learning and Training in Thornton Heath.

Her accomplishments also includes City & Guilds Basic English, a Diploma in Fine Art Ceramics, and a Pass in Fine Art AS level.

In 2007, at the age of 63, Muriel fulfilled her dream by publishing her first book, "The Two Little Mice and Mary-Ann." This was followed by several other titles: "Grandma's Ghost Story" in 2010, "Emily's Great Adventure" in 2013, "The Widow and the Vicar" in 2014, and "Once Upon a Farm" in 2022.

Ladies, gentlemen!
These poems were made for you.
Hope you enjoy them.

Snow dance lazily.
Breeze twirl softy in the night.
It is dark and cold.

Wet slippery ground.
Overnight frost hides black ice.
Look before you jump!

November morning.
Snowflakes linger in the air.
We hear robins sing.

White smoke dance all day,
out of an old wooden hut.
I stand still and gaze.

I cannot enter.
Snow drift noiselessly outside.
I watch in silence.

When the frost's over,
I'll meet you beyond the hill,
down by the river.

Oh mother, it's cold!
Everything frozen solid.
Can we go home now?

We walk in the dark.
The moon shines from behind the
cloud, to guide us home.

Oh, what a dim day.
It is wet, dark, damp and cold.
Let's get out of here.

The snow is heavy.
Draw curtains, light the fire.
Sit back and relax.

Cold sharp winter breeze.
Delightful fire burning.
Lovely hot cocoa.

Slow motion winter.
The nights are long, cold and dark.
I am nice and warm.

Cold, dark, damp, breezy.
Don't want to move painful joints.
Cold whispering wind.

With snow on her face,
she strides steadily through the
bitterly cold night.

Motionless winter.
Crystal clear icicles crash.
Beware! Walk safely!

She pulled her woolly
hat tight on her head, to keep
her warm. Gosh it's cold!

Night is dark and cold.
Wind is blowing hard and sharp.
Got to keep moving.

Glorious full moon,
risen high in the distance.
Guide me safely home.

Up and down people
walk, gazing where traffic flows.
Christmas bells ringing.

Over Putney bridge,
on either side traffic flows,
engines echo clear.

High street lights glitter.
Father Christmas jolly nice.
Children with bright eyes.

A warm bright Christmas,
somewhere in the West Indies.
Hummingbirds singing.

Green grass and sunlight.
Merriment lives in my soul.
A smile on my face.

I will make it back
to beautiful Jamaica,
to build me a house.

Caribbean food.
Jamaican national dish.
Ackee and saltfish.

Sweet is sugarcane,
so luscious, tall and handsome.
Dancing in the wind.

Delicious lunches.
Yam, sweet potatoes, dumplings,
spread out on green leaves.

On a moonless night,
the valley sleeps peaceful in
the silence of dark.

Down by the river,
when stars come out, we will walk
in the midnight breeze.

River winding through.
Lingering magic whisper.
People gazing out.

Morning has broken.
Unspoilt natural beauty.
Glorious sunrise.

Pancakes and syrup.
Delicious mouth-watering
appetizing food.

Glistening under
blanket of pure white soft snow,
crocus hurry out.

Winter is over.
There are raindrops and rainbows.
The sun is shining.

Apple buds are out.
Soon the honey bees will feed.
The birds are singing.

Spring will be here soon.
Time to start a new chapter.
A new beginning.

Spring

The young leaves are out.
Cold cruel winter is over.
The birds are singing.

Sweet scented blossom.
Lambs jumping in the meadow.
Mother smiles with joy.

A patchwork landscape.
Exhibitions of fine art.
Delightful display.

His bed was made of
natural straw, where he slept,
until the sun rose.

He got out of his
hut, to greet a lovely day
and watched the bees dance.

He drinks sweet coffee,
from an old enamel mug.
Very happy man.

Rivers and gullies
meander through the valleys,
to meet the great blue.

Stroll over wooden
footbridge, across open fields
and into the woods.

Green is springtime with
multicoloured trees swaying,
in the soft warm breeze.

Raindrops and rainbows.
Blackbirds sing, butterflies dance.
Happy children play.

All the world is young.
Green trees and yellow flowers
sway in the soft breeze.

In splendour they stand,
rooted deep beneath the ground.
Beautifully sweet.

Behind the narrow
gap of my white lace curtains,
I watch secretly.

He walks on my street,
with newspaper under arm.
I watch as he pass.

He stops, admires
my small beautiful garden,
not knowing I'm here.

Blow the winds of dusk,
warmly, softy, dreamingly,
till the morning comes.

Dewdrops and blossoms.
Glorious bright spring morning.
Blackbirds sing and dance.

Green is happiness,
a feeling of contentment.
Beautiful nature.

Soft April drizzle.
The sun is shining brightly.
I see the rainbows.

Poem in my head
and sweet music in my bones.
A smile on my face.

Mist covers mountains.
Apple trees bent with flowers.
Sunbeams warm the ground.

I stand in sunlight,
on the bank of the river.
Clear crystal water.

I watch with joy as
pleasant welcome breeze ripples
the water surface.

Meandering through
the wild dale, the river rest
deep beneath the rocks.

Cool night in April.
Raindrops on the window pane.
Shadows in the dark.

I love you, mama.
Today, tomorrow, always.
You are my sunshine.

Good night my darling.
Sleep sweet till the break of day.
Song birds sing wake up.

The cock crows at dawn.
Nightingales sing loud and clear.
Cows graze the sweet grass.

Thank the Universe,
for its magnificent gifts.
The sweet breath of life.

Beautiful meadows,
golden sunset, peaceful sea.
Unforgettable.

Sightseeing wonders.
Water cascading down rocks,
like strings of crystal.

Folks look up and down,
watching where the water flows
down the narrow stream.

I listen to the
sound of soft running water.
My thoughts drift away.

Gaze in amazement.
The wonderful landscape that
nature created.

I saw two magpies
on a branch high above me.
Two for joy, I thought.

Love is the greatest
gift on earth. Love is something
money cannot buy.

Summer

The nightingales sing
sweetly in the tall green tree.
Brings a cheerful day.

I gaze as the long
slender grass, sway endlessly,
in the soft warm breeze.

Beautiful woodland.

A surrounding countryside.

Amazing seashore.

Flowers by the road,
dancing in all directions.
Glorious raindrops!

Splashes and waggles.
Ripples dash across the lake.
Squawking ducks fly off.

With white wings displayed,
they gracefully fly away,
in the horizon.

He walks on the grass.
Down the steep hill he walks quick
to the water hole.

Sweetly and softly,
in my imagination,
he whispers my name.

He looks at the skies,
smiles warmly with happiness,
as he walks along.

The joy of beauty.
The adorable sweetheart.
The divine splendour.

Thinking of colour,
I see sunshine and blue skies.
I hear the birds sing.

In rainbow fashion,
magnificent waterfall
cascade over rocks.

Sunshine and blue sky.
Oh, what a glorious day.
Good day for picnic.

Mashed sweet potato,
surprisingly delicious.
Onions, butter, cheese.

With melted butter
dripping down between fingers,
how can I resist.

My dearest, rest with
me, in this peaceful garden,
till the dawn of day.

Garden of ripe fruit,
we rest under apple trees.
Whispering warm breeze.

Oh yes, my dearest,
as the sun, moon and stars shine,
my love lives always.

Sweet scented perfume.
Sweet lilies of the valley,
draw me closer still.

Under the pine trees,
we will sit, rest, eat and drink,
until morning comes.

The passion of love.
The dandelions dance for
happiness and peace.

Bees and butterflies
dancing, as they drink the sweet
juice from the flowers.

Beautiful summer.
Children with dirty faces,
building sand castles.

Scrumptious fish and chips,
dredged with salt and vinegar,
wrapped in newspaper.

The blistering sun,
scorching the dusty dry ground.
Rain is coming soon.

Whirlwind spins. Dust swerve.
Rooster scarpers for his life.
Dark clouds drift away.

Seagulls softy zoom,
high above the deep blue sea.
Outspread wings they glide.

Lightning and thunder!
Ice-cream splatter on pavement.
Frightened child runs fast.

Darkness and rainstorm.
Mysterious universe.
Weather-beaten ground.

The rain pounded down.
Clap of thunder. Wind wrestle
with the windowpane.

On Brighton sea front.
Cloudy night after the rain.
Calm after the storm.

Walking on seashore,
with pebbles beneath my feet,
I inhale cool air.

Softly and sweetly,
in my imagination,
the oak tree whispers.

It is harvest time.
The corn are ripe and ready.
Swallows twittering.

I step out into
my ever changing garden.
Autumn approaching.

Food for the hungry.
Delightful breathtaking scene.
Such wonderful taste.

Autumn

Come to my garden,
I am gathering ripe fruit.
How sweet is the day.

The pumpkins are big.
Almost ready to harvest.
Green, orange, yellow!

Tomatoes are ripe.
Some are still waiting to turn.
Last of summer's feast.

Moments of pleasure.
We walk hand in hand with joy.
The breeze blow softly.

Sky filled with grey clouds.
Time forever passing by.
Don't try to rush it.

Mornings are cooler.
There's a freshness in the air.
Changes are coming.

Black skirt, high-heeled shoes.
Tall lady walking swiftly.
There's a train to catch.

Skimming down the lane,
she sways side to side, watching
where the traffic flows.

The lightning flashed sharp,
thunder roared in the distance,
past the horizon.

The train's not moving.
Anxious passengers stand still.
Light's off. Hearts beats fast.

I'm sorry, but there's
an obstacle on the track,
announced the driver.

The light's on again.
Another five minutes pass.
At last, we are off.

I close the door to
hide from the world, so that I
may be left alone.

I walk quietly.
Slowly opened the curtains.
Flash of light came in.

The sun shines softly.
Through the window the breeze blows.
I am feeling good.

Nights getting cooler.
Strawberry leaves turning red.
Last of summer rays.

Preparing the earth
to plant onions and garlic,
ready for next year.

Gathering the twigs,
to set aside for winter.
Always be prepared.

Early morning walk,
in the warm golden sunrise,
onto open fields.

Stripped of their garments,
naked trees stand motionless.
Autumn breeze whispers.

Big fluffy pink clouds.
Birds flying in autumn sky.
Beautiful sunset.

Clocks one hour back.
Colourful leaves fall from trees.
Days getting shorter.

Mug of black coffee.
A large plate of fried plantain.
Mi gosh, food so sweet.

The sun peeking through
the dark cloud, then ready to
disappear again.

She left the warm room,
walked three paces to the door,
looked through the clear glass.

She opened the door
and nervously stepped outside,
whispering softly.

Golden leaves scatter.
Sharp breeze bruise fingers and lips.
Sun refused to smile.

The murmuring wind
rattles on the window pane.
Beats and bent the trees.

I am old and cold.
No fire to keep me warm.
Oh, if I were young.

Oh, you murmuring
breeze, why are you so restless?
It is time you sleep.

Flickering shadows.
Soft warm breeze, in the dark night.
Candle lights dancing.

The silence of sleep.
Everything is clam and still.
Whisper soft music.

Eight hours of sleep.
A good night of peaceful rest.
Feelings of refresh.

It's very frosty.
Robins hop to sip the dew.
Oh no, not a drop!

I close the window,
walk into the kitchen to
make a cup of tea.

Winter is coming.
Time for fluffy warm blankets.
Let's go hibernate.

You've come to the end.
I hope you feel inspired to
write your own haiku.